YOWL

Selected Poems About Cats

Illustrations by Ferris Cook

A Bulfinch Press Book

Little, Brown and Company

Boston · New York · London

Also available with illustrations by Ferris Cook

A Murmur in the Trees / Emily Dickinson
Bark: Selected Poems About Dogs / Various Poets
Odes to Common Things / Pablo Neruda
Odes to Opposites / Pablo Neruda
The Rose Window and Other Verse from New Poems / Rainer Maria Rilke
The Sonnets / William Shakespeare

First Edition

Library of Congress Cataloging-in-Publication Data
Yowl : selected poems about cats / [selections and] illustrations by Ferris
Cook.—1st ed.
   p. cm.
"A Bulfinch Press Book"
ISBN: 0-8212-2717-3
1. Cats—Poetry. I. Cook, Ferris
PN6110.C3 Y68 2001
808.81'93629752—dc21

                                                            2001029423

Bulfinch Press is an imprint and trademark of
Little, Brown and Company (Inc.)

Printed in the United States of America

For Norman, Sumiko, Alex, and Mr. Bean

CONTENTS

TO A CAT

Mirrors are not more wrapt in silences
nor the arriving dawn more secretive;
you, in the moonlight, are that panther figure
which we can only spy at from a distance.
By the mysterious functioning of some
divine decree, we seek you out in vain;
remoter than the Ganges or the sunset,
yours is the solitude, yours is the secret.
Your back allows the tentative caress
my hand extends. And you have condescended,
since that eternity, by now forgotten,
to take love from a flattering human hand.
You live in other time, lord of your realm —
a world as closed and separate as dream.

— Jorge Luis Borges

CAT

Old Mog comes in and sits on the newspaper
Old fat sociable cat
Thinks when we stroke him he's doing us a favour
Maybe he's right, at that.

— Joan Aiken

THE CAT TO HIS DINNER

Fern and flower, safely keep
this tender mouse I put to sleep.

Let snow and silence mark the site
of my unseemly appetite.

Her bravery, her tiny fall
shall be a model for us all.

May God, Who knows our best and worst,
send me another as good as the first.

— Nancy Willard

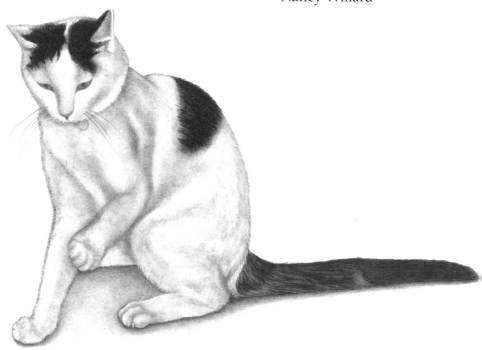

ODE TO THE CAT

There was something wrong
with the animals:
their tails were too long, and they had
unfortunate heads.
Then they started coming together,
little by little
fitting together to make a landscape,
developing birthmarks, grace, pep.
But the cat,
only the cat
turned out finished,
and proud:
born in a state of completion,
it sticks to itself and knows just what it wants.

Men would like to be fish or fowl,
snakes would rather have wings,
and dogs are would-be lions.
Engineers want to be poets,
flies emulate swallows,
and poets try hard to act like flies.
But the cat
wants nothing more than to be a cat,
and every cat is pure cat
from its whiskers to its tail,

from sixth sense to squirming rat,
from nighttime to its golden eyes.

Nothing hangs together
quite like a cat:
neither flowers nor the moon
have
such consistency.
It's a thing by itself,
like the sun or a topaz,
and the elastic curve of its back,
which is both subtle and confident,
is like the curve of a sailing ship's prow.
The cat's yellow eyes
are the only
slot
for depositing the coins of night.

O little
emperor without a realm,
conqueror without a homeland,
diminutive parlor tiger, nuptial
sultan of heavens
roofed in erotic tiles:
when you pass
in rough weather
and poise

four nimble paws
on the ground,
sniffing,
suspicious
of all earthly things
(because everything
feels filthy
to the cat's immaculate paw),
you claim
the touch of love in the air.

O freelance household
beast, arrogant
vestige of night,
lazy, agile
and strange,
O fathomless cat,
secret police
of human chambers
and badge
of
vanished velvet!
Surely there is nothing
enigmatic
in your manner,
maybe you aren't a mystery after all.
You're known to everyone, you belong

to the least mysterious tenant.
Everyone may believe it,
believe they're master,
owner, uncle
or companion
to a cat,
some cat's colleague,
disciple or friend.

But not me.
I'm not a believer.
I don't know a thing about cats.
I know everything else, including life and its archipelago,
seas and unpredictable cities,
plant life,
the women's room and its scandals,
the pluses and minuses of math.
I know the earth's volcanic protrusions
and the crocodile's unreal hide,
the fireman's unseen kindness
and the priest's blue atavism.
But cats I can't figure out.
My mind slides on their indifference.
Their eyes hold ciphers of gold.

— Pablo Neruda

#55

The cat doing kundalini
arches his back and
stretches up
doing the Flight of the Swan
with Leda looking on

— Lawrence Ferlinghetti

A CAT'S CONSCIENCE

A dog will often steal a bone,
But conscience lets him not alone,
And by his tail his guilt is known.

But cats consider theft a game,
And, howsoever you may blame,
Refuse the slightest sign of shame.

When food mysteriously goes,
The chances are that Pussy knows
More than she leads you to suppose.

And hence there is no need for you,
If Puss declines a meal or two,
To feel her pulse and make ado.

— Anonymous

SONNET TO A CAT

Cat! who hast pass'd thy grand climacteric,
  How many mice and rats hast in thy days
  Destroy'd? — How many tit bits stolen? Gaze
With those bright languid segments green, and prick
Those velvet ears — but pr'ythee do not stick
  Thy latent talons in me — and upraise
  Thy gentle mew — and tell me all thy frays
Of fish and mice, and rats and tender chick.
Nay, look not down, nor lick thy dainty wrists —
  For all the wheezy asthma, — and for all
Thy tail's tip is nick'd off — and though the fists
  Of many a maid have given thee many a maul,
Still is that fur as soft as when the lists
  In youth thou enter'dst on glass bottled wall.

—John Keats

THE KITTEN

The trouble with a kitten is
THAT
Eventually it becomes a
CAT.

— Ogden Nash

THE CAT AS CAT

The cat on my bosom
sleeping and purring
— fur-petalled chrysanthemum,
squirrel-killer —

is a metaphor only if I
force him to be one,
looking too long in his pale, fond,
dilating, contracting eyes

that reject mirrors, refuse
to observe what bides
stockstill.
        Likewise

flex and reflex of claws
gently pricking through sweater to skin
gently sustain their own tune,
not mine. I-Thou, cat, I-Thou.

— Denise Levertov

23

THE CATS

What the cats do
To amuse themselves
When we are gone
I do not know.
They have the yard
And the fences
Of the neighbors,
And, occasionally,
May arrive at the door, miaowing,
With drops of milk
On their chins,
Waving their shining tails
And exhibiting signs of alarm
When the light inside
The refrigerator
Goes on. But what
They do all day
Remains a mystery.
It is a dull neighborhood.
Children scream
From the playground.

The cars go by in a bluish light.
At six o'clock the cats run out
When we come home from work
To greet us, crying, dancing,
After the long day.

— Weldon Kees

LITTLE CATS

What happens to little cats?
    Some get drowned in a well,
    Some run over by a car —
    But none goes to hell.

What happens to little cats,
New born, not been here long?
    Some live out their
    Full nine lives —
As mean as they are strong.

— Langston Hughes

CATALOG

Cats sleep fat and walk thin.
Cats, when they sleep, slump;
When they wake, pull in —
And where the plump's been
There's skin.
Cats walk thin.

Cats wait in a lump.
Jump in a streak.
Cats, when they jump, are sleek
As a grape slipping its skin —
They have technique.
Oh, cats don't creak.
They sneak.

Cats sleep fat.
They spread comfort beneath them
Like a good mat,
As if they picked the place
And then sat.
You walk around one
As if he were the City Hall
After that.

If male,
A cat is apt to sing upon a major scale:
This concert is for everybody, this
Is wholesale.
For a baton, he wields a tail.

(He is also found,
When happy, to resound
With an enclosed and private sound.)

A cat condenses.
He pulls in his tail to go under bridges,
And himself to go under fences.
Cats fit
In any size box or kit;
And if a large pumpkin grew under one,
He could arch over it.

When everyone else is just ready to go out,
The cat is just ready to come in.
He's not where he's been.
Cats sleep fat and walk thin.

— Rosalie Moore

FOR A DEAF ANGORA CAT

The jungle lies about you, and the ground
Is measured by your stealthy step, the sound
Of birds extinct in pure, autumnal flight.
What centuries of breeding, ah, poor dear,
Brought you to your plight like aged Lear
Who struggled on the heath one winter night.

Enough. I follow you beyond the trees
Into the presence of your enemies,
The victims of your superhuman powers.
I find you on a plain whereon there dwell
The antelope, the ostrich, and gazelle,
And tall giraffe that might be speckled flowers.

A wind comes up from nowhere; grasses part
As if to announce a god, — there in the heart
Of darkness stands a Zulu with a spear.
We pay for purity: the heavens burn
With omens, thunder peals; and still you turn
To all, my sweet, your exquisite deaf ear.

— William Jay Smith

TO WINKY

Cat,
Cat,
What are you?
Son, through a thousand generations, of the black leopards
Padding among the sprigs of young bamboo;
Descendant of many removals from the white panthers
Who crouch by night under the loquat-trees?
You crouch under the orange begonias,
And your eyes are green
With the violence of murder,
Or half-closed and stealthy
Like your sheathed claws.
Slowly, slowly,
You rise and stretch
In a glossiness of beautiful curves,
Of muscles fluctuating under black, glazed hair.

Cat,
You are a strange creature.
You sit on your haunches
And yawn,
But when you leap
I can almost hear the whine
Of a released string,
And I look to see its flaccid shaking
In the place whence you sprang.

You carry your tail as a banner,
Slowly it passes my chair,
But when I look for you, you are on the table
Moving easily among the most delicate porcelains.
Your food is a matter of importance
And you are insistent on having
Your wants attended to,
And yet you will eat a bird and its feathers
Apparently without injury.

In the night, I hear you crying,
But if I try to find you
There are only the shadows of rhododendron leaves
Brushing the ground.
When you come in out of the rain,
All wet and with your tail full of burrs,
You fawn upon me in coils and subtleties;
But once you are dry
You leave me with a gesture of inconceivable impudence,
Conveyed by the vanishing quirk of your tail
As you slide through the open door.

You walk as a king scorning his subjects;
You flirt with me as a concubine in robes of silk.
Cat,
I am afraid of your poisonous beauty,
I have seen you torturing a mouse.
Yet when you lie purring in my lap
I forget everything but how soft you are,
And it is only when I feel your claws open upon my hand
That I remember —
Remember a puma lying out on a branch above my head
Years ago.

Shall I choke you, Cat,
Or kiss you?
Really I do not know.

— Amy Lowell

POEM

As the cat
climbed over
the top of

the jamcloset
first the right
forefoot

carefully
then the hind
stepped down

into the pit of
the empty
flowerpot

— William Carlos Williams

LUXURY

My cat, Pierrot
The eloquence
Of his sleep!
Tucked under
The ample breast
His paws
Are two velvet pillows
His thick-furred boots
Stretch out
In luscious abandon,
His colors are blue-gray
And silvery white.
His purrs lightly
Embroider the air.

No emerald,
No mink muff,
No ermine vest
Could provide
The luxury
Of this cat's sleep.
How rich I am!

— May Sarton

CATS

Lovers, scholars — the fervent, the austere —
grow equally fond of cats, their household pride.
As sensitive as either to the cold,
as sedentary, though so strong and sleek,

your cat, a friend to learning and to love,
seeks out both silence and the awesome dark . . .
Hell would have made the cat its courier
could it have controverted feline pride!

Dozing, all cats assume the svelte design
of desert sphinxes sprawled in solitude,
apparently transfixed by endless dreams;

their teeming loins are rich in magic sparks,
and golden specks like infinitesimal sand
glisten in those enigmatic eyes.

—Charles Baudelaire

THE TOM-CAT

At MIDNIGHT in the alley
  A Tom-cat comes to wail,
And he chants the hate of a million years
  As he swings his snaky tail.

Malevolent, bony, brindled,
  Tiger and devil and bard,
His eyes are coals from the middle of Hell
  And his heart is black and hard.

He twists and crouches and capers
  And bares his curved sharp claws,
And he sings to the stars of the jungle nights
  Ere cities were, or laws.

Beast from a world primeval,
  He and his leaping clan,
When the blotched red moon leers over the roofs
  Give voice to their scorn of man.

He will lie on a rug to-morrow
  And lick his silky fur,
And veil the brute in his yellow eyes
  And play he's tame, and purr.

But at midnight in the alley
  He will crouch again and wail,
And beat the time for his demon's song
  With the swing of his demon's tail.

— Don Marquis

WHAT THE WHISKERS MEASURE

A cat is a tamed wild thing,
or a wildly untamed daydream.
Pyramid-eared, square-shouldered,
she's feared by all the low-rollers:

crickets, weevils, mice, lizards —
yes, those little beings who quiver
when a cat turns hunter and creeps
along like a fever, then leaps!

A cat never squats: she sits
primly, self-contained, as if
what's poised within day's frame
is a feline portrait of dignity, fame.

What's best about a cat, though,
is a fact that few people know —
her whiskers span the width
of space through which she fits:

a thinnish cat's short whiskers
safely lead her through the briars,
while a plump cat's long moustache
keeps her sleuthing, unabashed.

— Maurya Simon

YOU KNOW HOW A CAT

will bring a mouse it has
caught and lay it at your

feet   so each morning I
bring you the poem that

I've written when I woke
up in the night as my tri-

bute to your beauty &
a promise of my love.

— James Laughlin

ON THE DEATH OF A CAT,
A FRIEND OF MINE, AGED
TEN YEARS AND A HALF

Who shall tell the lady's grief
When her Cat was past relief?
Who shall number the hot tears
Shed o'er her, beloved for years?
Who shall say the dark dismay
Which her dying caused that day?

Come, ye Muses, one and all,
Come obedient to my call.
Come and mourn, with tuneful breath,
Each one for a separate death;
And while you in numbers sigh,
I will sing her elegy.

Of a noble race she came,
And Grimalkin was her name.
Young and old full many a mouse
Felt the prowess of her house:
Weak and strong full many a rat
Cowered beneath her crushing pat:
And the birds around the place
Shrank from her too close embrace.
But one night, reft of her strength,
She laid down and died at length:

Lay a kitten by her side,
In whose life the mother died.
Spare her line and lineage,
Guard her kitten's tender age,
And that kitten's name as wide
Shall be known as her's that died.

And whoever passes by
The poor grave where Puss doth lie,
Softly, softly let him tread,
Nor disturb her narrow bed.

— Christina Rossetti

SHE SIGHTS A BIRD –
SHE CHUCKLES –

She sights a Bird — she chuckles —
She flattens — then she crawls —
She runs without the look of feet —
Her eyes increase to Balls —

Her Jaws stir — twitching — hungry —
Her Teeth can hardly stand —
She leaps, but Robin leaped the first —
Ah, Pussy, of the Sand,

The Hopes so juicy ripening —
You almost bathed your Tongue —
When Bliss disclosed a hundred Toes —
And fled with every one —

— Emily Dickinson

CAT & THE WEATHER

Cat takes a look at the weather.
Snow.
Puts a paw on the sill.
His perch is piled, is a pillow.

Shape of his pad appears.
Will it dig? No.
Not like sand.
Like his fur almost.

But licked, not liked.
Too cold.
Insects are flying, fainting down.
He'll try

to bat one against the pane.
They have no body and no buzz.
And now his feet are wet;
it's a puzzle.

Shakes each leg,
then shakes his skin
to get the white flies off.
Looks for his tail,

tells it to come on in
by the radiator.
World's turned queer
somehow. All white,

no smell. Well, here
inside it's still familiar.
He'll go to sleep until
it puts itself right.

— May Swenson

BLACK CAT

A ghost, though invisible, still is like a place
your sight can knock on, echoing; but here
within this thick black pelt, your strongest gaze
will be absorbed and utterly disappear:

just as a raving madman, when nothing else
can ease him, charges into his dark night
howling, pounds on the padded wall, and feels
the rage being taken in and pacified.

She seems to hide all looks that have ever fallen
into her, so that, like an audience,
she can look them over, menacing and sullen,
and curl to sleep with them. But all at once

as if awakened, she turns her face to yours;
and with a shock, you see yourself, tiny,
inside the golden amber of her eyeballs
suspended, like a prehistoric fly.

— Rainer Maria Rilke

CATNIP AND DOGWOOD

A cat's quite different from a dog
And you name it differently, too;
A library cat might be Catalogue,
And a Siamese, Fu Manchu.
Dogs usually have humdrum names
Like Molly, Blacky, Biff, and James.

Cats eat catnip excitedly,
Get drunk and jump around,
But a dog can sniff at a dogwood tree,
And sniff and sniff quite diligently,
Sit down and never budge —
And be as smug and sober as a judge.

— Howard Moss

CURIOSITY

may have killed the cat. More likely,
the cat was just unlucky, or else curious
to see what death was like, having no cause
to go on licking paws, or fathering
litter on litter of kittens, predictably.

Nevertheless, to be curious
is dangerous enough. To distrust
what is always said, what seems,
to ask odd questions, interfere in dreams,
smell rats, leave home, have hunches,
does not endear cats to those doggy circles
where well-smelt baskets, suitable wives, good lunches
are the order of things, and where prevails
much wagging of incurious heads and tails.

Face it. Curiosity
will not cause us to die —
only lack of it will.
Never to want to see
the other side of the hill

or that improbable country
where living is an idyll
(although a probable hell)
would kill us all.
Only the curious
have if they live a tale
worth telling at all.

Dogs say cats love too much, are irresponsible,
are dangerous, marry too many wives,
desert their children, chill all dinner tables
with tales of their nine lives.
Well, they are lucky. Let them be
nine-lived and contradictory,
curious enough to change, prepared to pay
the cat-price, which is to die
and die again and again,
each time with no less pain.
A cat-minority of one
is all that can be counted on
to tell the truth; and what cats have to tell
on each return from hell
is this: that dying is what the living do,
that dying is what the loving do,
and that dead dogs are those who never know
that dying is what, to live, each has to do.

— Alastair Reid

THE KILKENNY CATS

There wanst was two cats of Kilkenny,
Each thought there was one cat too many,
    So they quarrell'd and fit,
    They scratch'd and they bit,
    Till, barrin' their nails,
    And the tips of their tails,
Instead of two cats, there warnt any.

               — Anonymous

CREDITS

ACKNOWLEDGMENTS

My thanks to the following cats and their owners:

Mr. Bean (jacket, pp. v & 31): Norman, Sumiko & Alex Cook

Moby Dick (p. ii): Walter Chandoha

Tiger (pp. vi & 25): Gayle Saunders, Ethan, Max & Shelly Feldman

Daphne (p. viii): Emily & Steve Kane

Katia (p. 2): Evan Hill-Ries

Bibby (p. 4): Craig Leach & Kimberly Stephenson

Simon (pp. 6 & 7): Gail, Tim & Sheila Healy

Toonsis (pp. 9 & 13): Karin Anderson

The Lisbon Zoo (p. 15): Fafá Faria

Tina (p. 17): Mary Ellen & John Flemming

Lila (p. 19): Stephanie Speer

Zorro (p. 20): Gwen & Tom Hobson

Clyde (p. 21): Tana Miller & Janet Weissman

Amanda (p. 22): Elizabeth Easton

Peeps (p. 26): Craig Leach & Kimberly Stephenson

Puddy (p. 29): Tana Miller & Janet Weissman

Tuptin-Siamese Princess (p. 33): Dr. & Mrs. K. L. Krabbenhoft

Nachos (p. 35): Beth & Dan Saks

Nutty Smith (p. 37): Lillian James Smith

Phoebe (p. 39): Mary Ellen & John Flemming

Turbeau (p. 40): Linda & Jack Spyker-Oles

Murphy (p. 42): Everyone at The Corner Bookstore

Felix (p. 45): Diana Gongora & German Meneses

Cyndi (p. 47): Dawn Markle

Simon (p. 48): Diana Gongora

Max (p. 51): Mary Ellen & John Flemming

Satch (p. 52): Diana Gongora & German Meneses

Moo-Shu (p. 55): Ellen Scordato & Mark Rifkin

Goose (p. 56): Ann H. Kram

Muffin & Goose (p. 59): Ann Chase & John Ballantine

Clemmy (p. 60): Mary Ellen & John Flemming

Akira (p. 62): Sandi Zinaman, Dan & Galen Green

Bob (p. 64): Rich Rubin & Nancy Catandella

And thanks to my cousin Ann Ferris Rumage Fritschner for sending a twenty-minute tape recording of her cat C.J. (Charlotte Jordan) purring. It helped me understand what it is about cats. Thanks also to Walter Chandoha and Stan Ries, who were kind enough to let me use their professional photography for illustration.

As always, my friends at Bulfinch Press and Little, Brown have created a beautiful book: a special thanks to Dean Bornstein and Allison Kolbeck. There's a fine line between work and play, as any cat knows. On my end I've had a lot of play and hope the same is true for my editor, Karen Dane, because she's a pussycat. Most thanks to her for her catlike patience as I doggedly made last-minute additions.

Book design by Dean Bornstein
Printed by Meridian Printing, East Greenwich, Rhode Island
Bound by Acme Bookbinding, Charlestown, Massachusetts